100 Reasons
to be a
DEMOCRAT

By
Bruce Harris M.Ed

100 Reasons
to be a
DEMOCRAT

By
Bruce Harris M.Ed

Donkey Art on cover by Scott Lee

100 Reasons to be a DEMOCRAT
By Bruce Harris

1. We like spending other people's money

2. We are Pro-Abortion

3. We love Jimmy Carter

4. We represent the Confederacy and the History of White Supremacy

5. We got those pesky Indians out of the way.

6. We believe islands like Guam could tip over if it gets too populated.

7. We love freedom of speech, unless it isn't politically correct, or I just don't agree with it!

8. If we don't work, the state will take care of us.

9. If you want to marry your couch, no problem.

10. You can identify as a mermaid if that's how you feel.

11. We let everybody into America, even people that hate us. Yay multiculturalism!

12. If you're charged with murder you can live the rest of your life in jail with all sorts of amenities.

13. No more guns!

14. Enjoy our long waits for the doctor we choose for you!

15. No profiling,
even if they are
wielding a sword.

16. Punishments should be based on the color of the person you hurt.

17. We love Affirmative Action!

18. We like to talk it out with other nations who are bullies. It always works!

19. We like to choose which businesses to help, some call ~~it~~ it cronyism, we call it "government knows best".

20. We only think certain lives matter. Definitely no stinking pigs.

21. We have safe spaces for you, where you can suck your thumb and cry your little eyes out.

22. Everyone else is a racist.

23. Everyone else hates gays.

24. Everyone else is wrong and shouldn't be allowed to voice opinions.

25. Anyone can go into the girls' restroom as long as you wear a dress.

26. We have celebrities like Kim Kardashian and Whoopi!

27. We like to drive Priuses.

28. We are the definition of smug.

29. We control the media.

30. We are superior and like to let everyone know it.

31. We poop potpourri (Our shit don't stink).

32. We worship that little boy on MSNBC. Rachel something...

33. We will protest the right to protest.

34. We will also protest against protests.

35. We embrace hypocr~~is~~y.

36. If your opinion is different than ours, you're a fascist.

37. We have no idea how to vote, which is why we need armed Black Panthers at the polls.

38. We like our men with smug, self-satisfied beards.

39. We believe that America needs to cut back on the amount of toilet paper is used in one sitting.

40. We pass bills without reading them.

41. You can live in any of the **57** states!

42. Islamic terrorists don't exist. Just like God.

43. Our Supreme Leader, His Excellency, Al Gore, created the internet.

44. We don't vote, but when we do, it's more than once in the same election ...and by a dead guy.

45. Everyone is equal, except our leaders, they are more equal.

46. We are the 99%!

47. Our best friends are the trees.

48. Maybe in the future we will all live on collective farms. That's never gone wrong.

49. We see no need for history. It's just a buzzkill.

50. Communism works. It just hasn't been done the right way! Stalin and Mao were almost there.

51. No one owns anything. Feel free to live in any house you choose.

52. We don't pray or allow others to do it either.

53. We tax the rich and give to the poor, then tax the poor by holding lotteries.

54. Government has all the answers. We don't need to think for ourselves.

55. We have Cher!

56. We like to interpret the Constitution as we see fit.

57. Since we don't always have the most logical arguments, we yell. It works.

58. We are for higher wages.

And for raising the costs of businesses so they will have to fire those that get a higher wage.

59. We are the party that believes in Global Warming. Anyone who doesn't is a racist piece of poop.

60. We believe in the only true god, Obama.

61. As a democrat, we don't need a military. Diplomacy and appeasement always work. Just ask Chamberlain.

62. Those who break the law must receive the punishment, unless you're an illegal immigrant, you can do what you want.

63. We believe Israel can fend for itself. They don't have any enemies near them...

64. We think that the more you make, the more you give back, but where it goes, no one knows. We need a lock box.

65. We need regulations on everything that exists, including what people do in the bathroom of their own home.

66. We are the donkey party. There aren't any other names for donkeys, right?

67. We've had some amazing presidents like James Buchanan and Andrew Johnson.

68. We think the Electoral College should be eliminated. Popular vote rules!

69. We want to move to California and secede, because that'll work out.

70. Our motto is 'when in doubt, blame the Russians.'

71. Free Cellphones for everyone!

72. We love polls, because they are always correct. Ask Hillary.

73. We are self-righteous!

74. We have our hand out for some handouts.

75. Our government will help us get that fancy car we've always wanted.

76. We shouldn't leave a carbon footprint, so we'll never fly in a plane, drive a car, or turn on a light.

77. We have the support of Rosie O.

78. We have the unions in our pocket, our big fat lazy pocket.

79. We are with PETA, even if they euthanize thousands of animals a year.

80. We want wind energy! (unless it ruins our view)

81. Pretty-faced celebrities are on our side. They know best.

82. We love *Hamilton,* and its all-white cast.

83. We love the poor, even when we lock our car doors as we drive past them.

84. We only profile the police.

85. We are all a quarter Native American, right Ms. Warren?

86. We all know that Trump's policies are killing over 300 million Americans a year.

87. Its okay to flip flop, just like Obama and Hillary did on gay marriage.

88. We believed that it was wise to put Japanese-Americans in camps back in WWII. FDR wouldn't do something immoral?!

89. We don't want a wall on our country's border, just a wall around our neighborhoods and homes.

90. We believe Benghazi was caused by a racist video.

91. We think Sharia Law is more practical than the Constitution.

92. We are for tolerance, unless you are a white Christian.

93. So what if we were the party of slavery?!

94. So what if we were the founding party of the KKK?!

95. We know which light bulbs people should use. Ones with mercury in them.

96. We know our education system is doing just fine. That's what the Teachers Unions are telling us...

97. We believe that smoking cigarettes is wrong, and if you smoke you are a fascist pariah who shouldn't be allowed in America.

98. Republicans didn't free the slaves... wait, they did?

99. We are the party against flags and statues.

100. We will control all aspects of everyone's life!

Proof

Made in the USA
Columbia, SC
02 September 2017